OLD SWORD-PLAY

Techniques of the Great Masters

Yours very Truly
Alfred Hutton

OLD SWORD-PLAY
Techniques of the Great Masters

BY

ALFRED HUTTON

WITH A NEW FOREWORD BY

Maestro Ramón Martínez

President, Association for Historical Fencing
Founding Member, International Masters at Arms Federation

DOVER PUBLICATIONS, INC.
Mineola, New York

Bibliographical Note

This Dover edition, first published in 2001, is an unabridged republication of the work first published as *Old Sword-Play: The Systems of Fence in Vogue During the XVIth, XVIIth, and XVIIIth Centuries, with Lessons Arranged from the Works of Various Ancient Masters* by H. Grevel & Co., London, and B. Westermann & Co., New York, in 1892.

For this edition, the Foreword by Ramón Martínez has been added, and minor changes have been made: printer's marks have been deleted, some running heads have been added, and all pages have been numbered.

Dover Publications wishes to thank Mr. Steve Hick for his valuable assistance in preparing this book for publication.

Library of Congress Cataloging-in-Publication Data

Hutton, Alfred.
    Old Sword Play : techniques of the great masters / Alfred Hutton ; foreword by Ramon Martinez.
        p. cm.
    Originally published: London : H. Grevel ; New York : B. Westermann, 1892.
    ISBN 0-486-41951-7 (pbk.)
    1. Swordplay. 2. Fencing. I. Title.
U865 .H89 2001
796.86—dc21

                                                                2001047482

Manufactured in the United States of America
Dover Publications, Inc., 31 East 2nd Street, Mineola, N.Y. 11501

FOREWORD TO DOVER EDITION

One often hears that history repeats itself, and that things come in cycles. Within the last few years, there has been an incredible resurgence of international interest in the methods and techniques of the swordsmanship of past ages. Over a hundred years ago, in Victorian England, there was a similar resurgence of interest. Captain Alfred Hutton, along with his colleagues Egerton Castle and Sir Richard Francis Burton, was in the forefront of the movement to revive the art of the sword in England. To this end, he traveled and lectured widely, giving fencing demonstrations throughout the country. His massive library was later bequeathed to the Victoria and Albert Museum.

Like many of his contemporaries, Hutton was a polymath: a career military officer, an antiquarian, and a teacher of swordsmanship. These three interests converged in his works, which sought to reintroduce realistic swordsmanship to a country that had ceased to resort to steel as a means of settling private quarrels. Hutton argued that for military men, training in the art and science of fencing was essential, as, at that time, such individuals might still be called upon to use their swords in the field of battle. In his *Cold Steel* (1889), for instance, he gives instruction in the use of saber, dueling sword, bayonet, great stick, truncheon, and dagger. Hutton, however, augmented the classical French technique in which he had been schooled with techniques drawn from masters of the past. The elegant and deadly eighteenth-century smallsword of Angelo, the seventeenth-century rapier and dagger of Alfieri, and Marozzo's sixteenth-century unarmed defenses against a man with a dagger, plainly fascinated him.

Hutton's contribution to the study of historical fencing found its culmination in 1892 with the publication of *Old Sword-Play*, a manual that presented "the systems of fence in use during the xvith, xviith, and xviiith centuries." By presenting the work of the ancient masters in a form comprehensible to the swordsmen of his own day, Hutton upheld the idea that true swordsmanship is always, and has been always, practical. He also sought to rekindle interest in fencing amongst his countrymen, which had almost disappeared by the latter half of the nineteenth century. We may speculate that Victorian England's interest in all things antiquarian, especially things having to do with the preindustrial world, led to Hutton's success in this venture.

It must be borne in mind, however, that this flagging interest in swordsmanship was the case only in England. In contemporary France, Spain, and Italy, there were still masters who taught some of the ancient skills. The baron de Bazancourt, in his *Secrets of the Sword* (1862), relates his meeting with an Italian fencing master who was well-versed in rapier and dagger. Likewise, Burton, in his *Sentiment of the Sword* (published posthumously in 1911), tells how the Italians adhered to their old practices, such as training outdoors (in contrast to the French, whose custom was to practice only indoors). Egerton Castle, before writing his monumental work *Schools and Masters of Fence* (1884), made a specific point of traveling to Italy to study with contemporary Neapolitan masters who retained in their teachings many of the theories and principles of the Italian rapier play of the sixteenth and seventeenth centuries, particularly in the use of the unarmed hand and auxiliary weapons such as the dagger.

It may flatter many of those who are now engaged in the study and practice of the historical forms of European swordsmanship to think that they are the first to take a serious approach to this subject, and that their views, expressed today, are unique. However, a close perusal of these pioneering works will reveal that over a hundred years ago, professional swordsmen had made the very same observations. There is, indeed, nothing new under the sun when it comes to the art of the sword.

In the late nineteenth century, fencing embodied a paradox. In one respect, as an art form, recreational pursuit, and gentlemanly accomplishment, it achieved a sort of Golden Age of perfection of form. On the other hand, it was also practical preparation for military service, and on the continent, for private duels. It is ironic that, at the exact moment in time that fencing both reached this stage of refinement and began to wane from practical use, interest in historical weapons began to flourish as never before.

Today fencing has become divorced from the grim realities of violent encounters in earnest, in which life and limb are actually at risk. Given that swords today are even more completely obsolete as practical weapons than they were in Hutton's day, the good captain's observations are, if anything, all the more poignant.

It is my hope that this new edition of *Old Sword-Play* will contribute to the new renaissance of the exercise of arms. It is with great joy that I, as a teacher of the art and science of fencing, have been involved in reintroducing Captain Hutton and his work to the world. I hope that today's readers will find it to be as important and valuable a work as it was then.

Maestro Ramón Martínez
President, Association for Historical Fencing
Founding member, International Masters at Arms Federation

PREFACE.

THE ensuing lessons on "Old Sword-Play" have been compiled from the works of various authors of the sixteenth, seventeenth, and eighteenth centuries; and it has been my intention so to arrange them as to make the antique methods accessible to the student without the labour of searching the pages of books in various languages, many of which are very difficult to procure, and much more so to understand. There are those who affect to ridicule the study of obsolete weapons, alleging that it is of no practical use; everything, however, is useful to the Art of Fence which tends to create an interest in it, and certain it is that such contests as " Rapier and Dagger," "Two-hand Sword," or " Broadsword and Handbuckler," are a very great embellishment to the somewhat monotonous proceedings of the ordinary "assault of arms."

The " Combinations " will be found extremely useful as forms of "set play" for combats on the dramatic stage.

I presuppose that, before turning his attention to the swordsmanship of bygone centuries, our student will have made himself reasonably proficient in the use of the modern arms—the foil and the sabre—under the tuition of some competent master.

ALFRED HUTTON.

CONTENTS.

LIST OF PLATES.

CHAPTER I.

INTRODUCTION.

HE Art of Fencing, in Europe, has seen four distinct periods, during which it has been influenced partly by the forms of the weapons, and partly, for the arms themselves were so influenced, by the changing fashions in dress. We find first the Shakespearian or Tudor era—that of the sixteenth century—when owing to the prevailing style of costume, and to the fact that the swords were long and unwieldy, they were almost always accompanied by an arm either purely defensive, like the buckler or the cloak, or by one, such as the dagger, of a character at once defensive and offensive ; these auxiliary arms were carried in the left hand, and their movements were extremely simple.

The second period, and perhaps the most interesting of them all, that of the Stuarts, was a period of transition ; the dagger had passed out of fashion as an article of dress, and in Western Europe the long, handsome rapier had by degrees given place to the short walking sword, which, however, did not assume a settled form until the century following ; but the Italians, who were the original teachers of our art, adhered to the earlier form. This change of pattern in the sword necessitated a change in the method of using it, and hence arose the two great and only "schools" of fence, the Italian and the French.

From this point we deal with the French system alone, and we find that as the short, light swords improved in their form, the art of wielding them advanced in precision and grace, which latter quality may be said to have attained its perfection about the middle of the eighteenth century, at the time, in fact, when the first of the Angelos brought out his famous folio. In the works of this period there is a very noticeable feature in the numerous tricks which the masters taught their pupils for depriving an enemy of his sword. In this our modern time disarming is not usually allowed, and it is always considered very rough play; but in the days of which we speak the sword was an integral part of every gentleman's dress, and a facility in disarming no doubt saved many a life in the sudden quarrels in street or tavern which were then matters of every-day occurrence.

About the middle of the last century wire fencing masks were introduced, but there was a feeling against them on the part of the masters, and it was some considerable time before they came into general use; previous to their adoption a fencing bout bore a somewhat stately and academic aspect— the movements were slow, and it was a matter of etiquette not to *riposte* until after the adversary had recovered from his lunge, for fear of injuring his face. All this, however, was altered about the beginning of this century, when the attitude of the masters towards the mask was changed by a serious accident which happened to one of them, and under the auspices of such men as Jean Louis, Gomard, Cordelois, and others, not to mention many famous teachers of the present day, the art of point-fencing has attained its climax.

CHAPTER II.

THE TWO-HAND SWORD.

THIS weapon, sometimes known as the old English "long sword," as a fighting arm stands by itself; it was the favourite weapon of our King Henry VIII. in his athletic days, and he proposed its use in the tournaments at the "Field of the Cloth of Gold," but Francis I. objected to it on the ground that there were no gauntlets then made sufficiently strong to guarantee the hands against its powerful strokes.

The following lessons have been compiled from the works of Marozzo (1536), Di Grassi (1570), Joachim Meyer (1570), Jacob Sutor (1612), and Alfieri (1653). The method of handling the weapon is very similar to the exercises of the "Great Stick," introduced in 1889 in "Cold Steel," and adapted from Italian sources; in fact, these latter are a distinct survival of the two-hand sword-play of the sixteenth century. The best manner of carrying the two-hander is taken from Alfieri (Plate 1). It is borne point upwards in the left hand, which grasps the grip about the centre, with the flat of the blade resting against the shoulder; it must be remembered that this sword is double edged.

TO SALUTE.

1. Pass the right hand across the body and seize the grip close to the quillons.

2. Bring the sword perpendicularly in front of the body with the quillons in line with the mouth.

3. Carry the sword over to the right side, and lower the point to the front about four inches from the ground, and draw back the right foot about six inches.

4. Raise the sword to a perpendicular position at the right side.

5. Carry the sword over to the left side, and resume the marching position.

GUARDS.

The favourite engaging guard of Marozzo was his *guardia di testa*, as seen in the illustration (Plate 2). Alfieri also makes use of one very similar. The guards in *quarte—porta di ferro alta*—(Plate 3), and *tierce—coda lunga e stretta*—(Plate 4), may also be used.

THE CUTS.

There are six principal cuts: two oblique downwards at the sides of the head or the shoulders, two oblique upwards, and two horizontal cuts, made usually at the flank. Those delivered at the left side of the enemy were called *mandritti*, and those at his right side *riversi*; the former were given with the right foot, and the latter with the left foot in advance.

THE MOULINETS.

The six moulinets are absolutely necessary for the acquirement of dexterity in wielding the two-hander; and in practising them great care must be taken to keep the hands well advanced, in order to avoid the accident of entangling the arms with the long quillons of the sword. They are as follows:—

Moulinet 1.

Motion 1.—Extend the arms with the sword pointing to the front a little above the diagonal line 1 on the target, the right hand holding it close to the quillons and the left hand close to the pummel.

Motion 2.—Bring the sword down, true edge leading, with a circular sweep from right to left along the line, causing it to pass close to the left side, and completing the circle bring it again to the front.

Moulinet 2.

Motion 1.—Extend the arms as before, the point of the sword being just above diagonal line 2.

Motion 2.—Describe a similar circle, the point traversing the diagonal line from left to right, and passing close to the right side.

Moulinet 3.

Motion 1.—Extend the arms and sword with the point directed just below line 3.

Motion 2.—Make the cut diagonally upwards, and, after the sword has passed through the target, complete the circle close to the right side.

Moulinet 4.

This must be performed as the last, save that the sword describes its circle close to the left side and passes diagonally upwards from left to right.

MOULINET 5.

Motion 1.—Extend the arms and sword with the point just outside line 5.

Motion 2.—Describe the circle horizontally, the sword traversing the line from right to left, and in the rearward half of the circle just clearing the top of the head.

MOULINET 6.

This must be executed similarly to the last, the sword describing the circle from left to right.

N.B.—The rotary movement of the sword is much assisted by a pulling motion with one hand and a pushing one with the other.

THE PARRIES.

For practical purposes it is better to substitute modern names for the obsolete and inconvenient terms used by the old writers, as—

Quarte	for " Porta di ferro alta."	(Plate 3.)
Tierce	,, " Coda lunga e stretta."	(Plate 4.)
Septime	,, " Porta di ferro larga."	(Plate 5.)
Seconde	,, " Becha cesa."	(Plate 6.)
Prime	,, " Becha possa."	(Plate 7,)
High Octave	,, " Intrare in largo passo."	(Plate 8.)

In the two latter the hands should be raised higher and the point dropped lower than in the woodcuts in Marozzo's work.

ON THE LEFT SIDE.

Quarte—parries cut 1 at the left cheek or shoulder.

Low Quarte—parries cut 5 at the left side.

High Quarte—parries a " stramazzone " or vertical cut at the left part of the head.

Septime—parries a cut at the legs on the left side.

ON THE RIGHT SIDE.

Tierce—parries cut 2 at the right cheek, etc.

Low Tierce—parries cut 6 at the right side.

High Tierce—parries the "stramazzone" at the right part of the head.

Seconde—parries a cut at the legs on the right side.

Prime and *High Octave* are auxiliary parries for *ripostes* given over the sword, at the left and right sides of the head respectively.

COMBINATIONS.

As soon as a knowledge of the parries and facility in performing the moulinets has been acquired, the following combinations should be carefully practised ; they will be found useful as a form of "set play" in stage combats or assaults of arms, and, indeed, the weapons are so dangerously heavy that on such occasions "set" is more to be recommended than "loose" play.

COMBINATION 1.

M. commences, advancing pass by pass, and making the six cuts at P., who retires pass by pass, and forming the six parries.

Reverse the practice.

COMBINATION 2.

M.	P.
Cut 1.	Parry Quarte, cut 2 over.
High Octave.	

Reverse the practice.

COMBINATION 3.

Cut 2.	Tierce, cut 1 over.
Prime.	

Reverse the practice.

COMBINATION 4.

Cut 1.
High Octave, cut 6.
Prime.

Quarte, cut 2 over.
Low Tierce, cut 1 over.

Reverse the practice.

COMBINATION 5.

Cut 1.
High Octave, cut 2.
Low Quarte.

Quarte, cut 4 under.
Tierce, cut 5.

Reverse the practice.

COMBINATION 6.

Cut 2.
Prime, cut 5.
High Octave.

Tierce, cut 1 over.
Low Quarte, cut 2 over.

Reverse the practice.

COMBINATION 7.

Cut 3.
Quarte, cut 6.
Prime.

Septime, cut 1.
Low Tierce, cut 1 over.

Reverse the practice.

COMBINATION 8.

Cut 4.
Tierce, cut 5 under.
High Octave.

Seconde, cut 2.
Low Quarte, cut 2 over.

Reverse the practice.

PLATE 1.

Two-Hand Swordsman Marching. *After Alfieri,* 1653.

PLATE 2.

THE ENGAGING GUARD. *After Marozzo.*

"Porta di Ferro Alta" (Quarte). *After Marozzo.*

PLATE 4.

"Coda Lunga e Stretta" (Tierce). *After Marozzo.*

"PORTA DI FERRO LARGA" (SEPTIME). *After Marozzo.*

"Becha Cesa" (Seconde). *After Marozzo.*

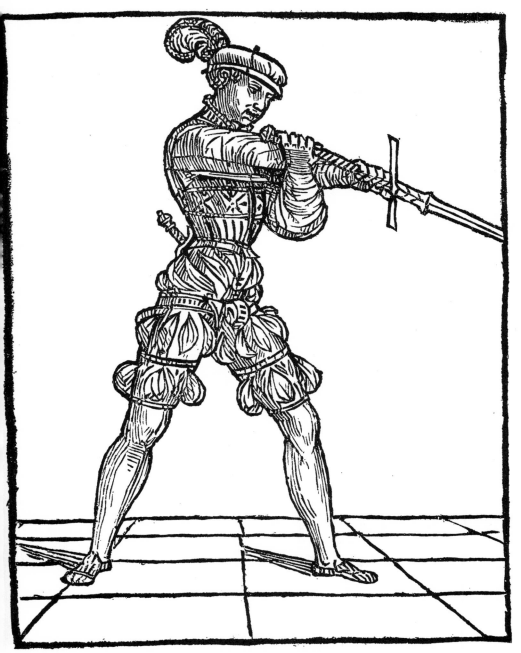

"Becha Possa" (Prime). *After Marozzo.*

PLATE 8.

"Intrare in Largo Passo" (High Octave). *After Marozzo.*

CHAPTER III.

RAPIER AND DAGGER.

HE Fence of the Rapier and Dagger takes, with regard to other arms of the period, a place similar to that occupied at the present time by that of the foil, being the most complete development of the various systems in which an auxiliary weapon was carried in the left hand; and undoubtedly a man fairly well skilled in it can master, with but little difficulty, the somewhat earlier exercises of " Sword and Buckler," " Sword (or dagger) and Cloak," and even the more puzzling " Case of Rapiers," in which a pair of swords, much of the type of those used in buckler-play, were carried, one in each hand.

The rapier, a long double-edged weapon, with ample " quillons " and " counterguards," which latter afterwards assumed the form of a cup, was held in the right hand with the forefinger crossed over the " quillon." In early times the edges were undoubtedly used, but they were by degrees abandoned in favour of the swifter and more deadly point. In our revival of this practice, therefore, we shall adhere to pure point-play, and we shall reserve that of the edge for the sword and buckler, in which it plays the most important part.

The dagger was held in the left hand, point upwards, with the thumb extended and resting in the spoon-shaped cavity in the forte of the blade. The dagger was used for parrying the thrusts of the sword, and was but sparingly employed in attack.

THE GUARDS.

The guards were four in number; they were simply positions of the sword from which attacks were made, and they were formed with either the right or the left foot advanced.

Prime—is the first position which the hand naturally assumes immediately after drawing the sword, the hilt being held above the head, the edge upwards, and the point towards the enemy (Plate 9).

Seconde—the hand is in pronation at the level of the shoulder, the arm being a good deal extended and the point level (Plate 9).

Tierce—the hand is about as high as the waist, in pronation, with the point in line with the opponent's face, and the edge directed obliquely downwards towards the right (Plate 10).

Quarte—the hand is at the height of the waist, in supination, the point in line with the opponent's face (Plate 10).

Alfieri introduced a medium guard, *Guardia Mista*, which assumed a middle position between Tierce and Quarte (Plate 11).

PLATE 9.

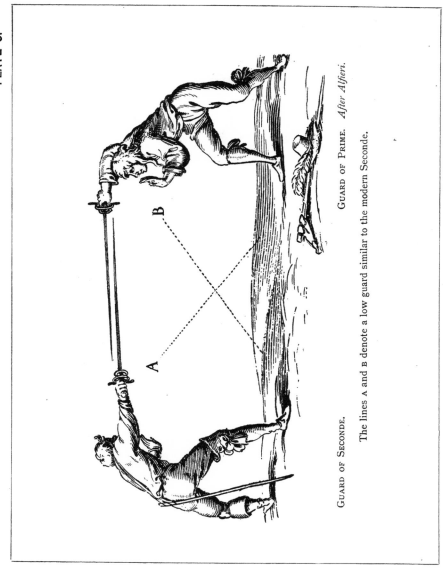

GUARD OF PRIME. *After Alfieri.*

GUARD OF SECONDE.

The lines A and B denote a low guard similar to the modern Seconde.

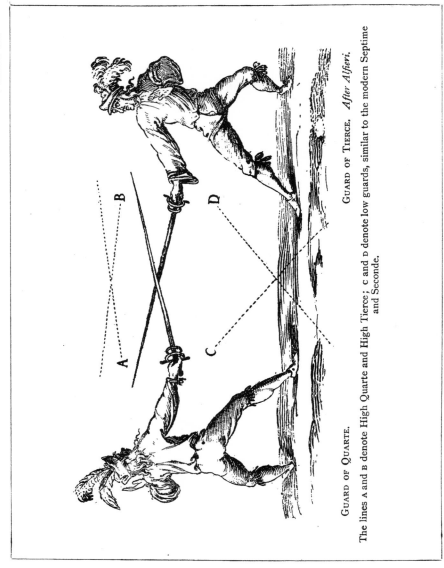

PLATE 10.

GUARD OF QUARTE.

GUARD OF TIERCE. *After Alfieri.*

The lines A and B denote High Quarte and High Tierce; C and D denote low guards, similar to the modern Septime and Seconde.

PLATE 11.

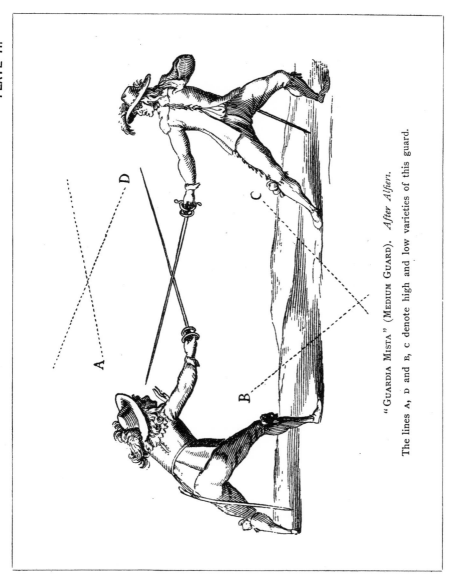

"Guardia Mista" (Medium Guard). *After Alfieri.*

The lines A, D and B, C denote high and low varieties of this guard.

THE THRUSTS.

The thrusts were—

Imbroccata—given from the Prime position above the enemy's dagger.

Stoccata—under the dagger.

Punta riversa—an exaggerated form of Quarte thrust, given either outside the enemy's sword or between his weapons.

These attacks were delivered either without moving the feet at all, or with the pass, or else with the " botta lunga " or lunge, as occasion might require.

FEINTS.

The feints were very few in number, because with the dagger only the simplest form of parry could be used ; they were " under and over " (Plate 16), and " over and disengage " (Plate 12), striking in the middle, between the weapons.

THE PARRIES.

The parries with the dagger were *Tierce* (Plate 16) for the high outside, *Seconde* for the low outside, *High Quarte* for the high inside, and *Low Quarte* (Plate 14) for the low inside.

The dagger is also used for " commanding " the enemy's sword in any of the four positions.

In a "corps à corps" it is sometimes useful to suddenly drop the rapier, and with the right hand to seize the left hand of the opponent, striking him instantly with the dagger.

COMBINATIONS.

M. P.

COMBINATION 1.

Thrust over the dagger.　　Parry Tierce, thrust under.
Seconde.

COMBINATION 2.

Thrust between the weapons.　Low Quarte, thrust in Prime
Tierce.　　　　　　　　　　over.

COMBINATION 3.

Thrust under.　　　　　　　Parry Seconde, thrust under.
Seconde.　·　　　　　　　　Pass, and give the dagger.

COMBINATION 4.

Thrust high between the　　Parry High Quarte, thrust
　weapons.　　　　　　　　low.
Seconde.　　　　　　　　　Pass, and give the dagger.

PLATE 12.

OVER AND DISENGAGE. *After Alfieri.*

The line A shows the feint, and the line B gives an alternate thrust at the breast.

PLATE 13.

COMMANDING THE BLADE WITH THE DAGGER IN TIERCE. *After Alfieri.*

The line A gives an alternative "riverso" at the head, B a low thrust, and C a "mandritto" at the leg.

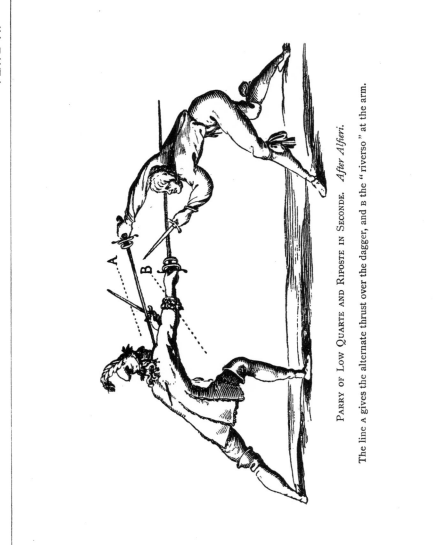

PLATE 14.

Parry of Low Quarte and Riposte in Seconde. *After Alfieri.*

The line A gives the alternate thrust over the dagger, and B the "riverso" at the arm.

PLATE 15.

PARRY OF HIGH QUARTE AND RIPOSTE UNDER THE ARM. *After Alfieri.*

The line A gives the alternative of a thrust at the face, and B that of a "mandritto" at the leg.

PLATE 16.

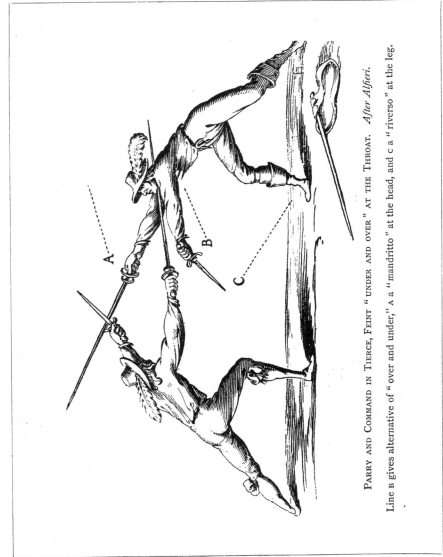

PARRY AND COMMAND IN TIERCE, FEINT "UNDER AND OVER" AT THE THROAT. *After Alfieri.*

Line B gives alternative of "over and under," A a "mandritto" at the head, and c a "riverso" at the leg.

CHAPTER IV.

BROADSWORD AND BUCKLER.

THIS exercise is considerably older than that of the long rapier and dagger, before which weapons it speedily vanished.

The Sword was a somewhat short one, and double edged. Cuts were given with either true or false edge, but the point was rarely used; it was held, like the rapier, with the forefinger over the cross-guard.

The Buckler, a small round shield, at the most some fourteen inches in diameter, was held in the left *fist*, and was not allowed in any way to rest on the arm; and when it was furnished with a spike, the spike was used for stabbing at close quarters.

THE GUARD.

The combatants engaged with the left foot forward and the buckler held in front of the body, with the arm extended, but not stiff, while the sword hand must be kept closer to the body, and somewhat under the shelter of the buckler (Plate 17.)

Marozzo gives twelve guards or positions of the sword
for attack, which, when assumed consecutively, are known as
" progressions."   These movements are extremely picturesque,
and should be performed at an " Assault of Arms" previously
to commencing the combat.   When there are four combatants,
A, B, C, and D, they should take their places at the four
corners of the stage, A and B occupying those nearest to
the audience.   At a signal from A, from whom they will
take their time, they will step forth with the *right foot*, and
advance towards the centre, A meeting D, and B meeting C.

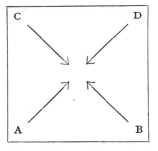

At each step a guard is to be formed as laid down below ;
and when the four meet in the centre they will salute each
one his opposite, by raising the sword-hilt in line with the
mouth, and then extending the sword *very high* to the front,
with the arm quite straight, so that all the points shall
cross in the centre.   After this they will lower their points,
step back one pace, and at the same time give two beats
on the buckler with the back of the sword, when A will
engage B near the audience, and C will engage D farther
back ; and when this time is up the Marshal, or M.C., will
stop C and D first, and will proceed, accompanied by them,
to stop A and B, on which all four will retire together.

PLATE 17.

ENGAGING GUARD. *After Marozzo.*

THE PROGRESSIONS OF MAROZZO.

1. *Coda lunga e stretta* . Right foot forward, hand in quarte, buckler extended. (Plate 18.)

2. *Cinghiara porta di ferro*   Left foot forward, hand in low tierce, buckler close to the face. (Plate 19.)

3. *Guardia alta*   .   . Right foot forward, arm extended high to the right, buckler extended. (Plate 20.)

4. *Coda lunga ed alta* . Left foot forward, hand in low tierce, buckler extended to left front. (Plate 21.)

5. *Porta di ferro stretta* . Right foot forward, hand in low quarte, buckler close to the face. (Plate 22.)

6. *Coda lunga e distesa* . Left foot forward, arm extended low to the right, buckler extended to the left. (Plate 23.)

7. *Guardia di testa* .   . Right foot forward, point raised to the front in high tierce, buckler low and centred. (Plate 24.)

8. *Guardia di intrare*   .   Left foot passed to left front, arm extended in supination, buckler to left front. (Plate 25.)

9. *Coda lunga e larga*   .   Right foot forward, hand down as in modern salute. (Plate 26.)

10. *Becha possa* .   .   .   Left foot forward, sword extended rather to the right in the form of the hanging guard. (Plate 27.)

11. *Guardia di facia* .   .   Right foot forward, arm extended to the front in supination. (Plate 28.)

12. *Becha cesa* .   .   .   Right foot forward, arm extended rather to the right in the position of the hanging guard. (Plate 29.)

When the sword is advanced the buckler is drawn in, and *vice versâ*.

N.B.—There appears to have been an error on the part of the artist in " becha cesa "; judging from the text the left foot should be advanced instead of the right.

PLATE 18.

"·Coda Lunga· e Stretta." *After ·Marozzo.*

PLATE 19.

" Cinghiara Porta di Ferro."   *After Marozzo.*

PLATE 20.

"Guardia Alta." *After Marozzo.*

PLATE 21

"Coda Lunga ed Alta." *After Marozzo.*

PLATE 22.

"Porta di Ferro Stretta, o Vera Larga." *After Marozzo.*

"Coda Lunga e Distesa." *After Marozzo.*

In this plate there has been a mistake on the part of the original artist—according to the text the left leg should be in advance.—A. H.

PLATE 24.

"Guardia di Testa." *After Marozzo.*

"Guardia di Intrare." *After Marozzo.*

PLATE 26.

"Coda Lunga e Larga." *After Marozzo.*

"Becha Possa." *After Marozzo.*

PLATE 28.

"Guardia di Facia."   *After Marozzo.*

PLATE 29.

"Becha Cesa." *After Marozzo.*

THE ATTACK.

The attack is made by cuts with either edge, but it is better to avoid the use of the point. It is made either without moving the feet or on the pass, but *never* on the lunge, for in the days when it was practised the lunge had not been invented.

There are six principal cuts, as in modern play, three being "mandritti" and three "riversi":—

1. Oblique downwards from right to left.
2. Oblique downwards from left to right.
3. Oblique upwards from right to left.
4. Oblique upwards from left to right.
5. Horizontal from right to left.
6. Horizontal from left to right.

The stramazzone, or vertical cut, is sometimes employed.

The false edge can be used with cut 1 at the back of the neck, cut 5 at the left side or back part of the left arm, or with cut 3, which is delivered at the back part of the left ham, when it is known as the "coup de Jarnac."

The true edge cuts 3 and 4, at or below the knee, we do not permit, on account of the danger of inflicting serious injury.

PARRIES.

It is as well to designate the defensive movements of the buckler by modern terms, thus :—

Tierce—parries cut 1, by raising the buckler to the left front.

Quarte—parries cut 2, by raising it to the right front.

Seconde—parries cut 3, by dropping it to the left front.

Septime—parries cut 4, by dropping it to the right front.

The cuts 5 and 6 are parried by low tierce and low quarte. The "coup de Jarnac" is best met by passing back the left foot, parrying seconde, and at the same time delivering a vertical cut at the forearm.

The converse of the above must be observed when the fencer is left-handed.

COMBINATIONS.

M.   P.

COMBINATION 1.

Cut 1.   Parry Tierce, cut 1.
Parry Tierce, cut 5.   Low Tierce, cut 2.
Parry Quarte.

COMBINATION 2.

Cut 2.   Parry Quarte, Coup de Jarnac.
Parry Seconde, cut 5.   Low Tierce, cut 2.
Parry Quarte.

COMBINATION 3.

Coup de Jarnac.   Parry Seconde, cut 1.
Parry Tierce, cut 5.   Low Tierce, cut 2.
Parry Quarte.

CHAPTER V.

RAPIER AND CLOAK.

N this exercise the Cloak takes the place, as a defensive weapon, of the buckler or the dagger. It must be turned twice round the left arm in such a manner as to cover the elbow, while the collar is grasped in the left hand; the ends are to be passed over the arm so as to hang down in folds on the outside of it, and with these folds (never with the part which rests on the arm) the various attacks are parried (Plate 30.)

THROWING THE CLOAK.

It is sometimes advisable to throw the cloak over either the face or the sword of the enemy. Marozzo's directions for doing this are as follows :—

Stand with the sword in low tierce (*coda lunga ed alta*), feign two or three thrusts at him while you are freeing the folds of your cloak, then pass the point of your sword underneath it, and with the assistance of the sword toss it either on to his face or his sword (Plate 32.)

Swordsmen of the olden time occasionally carried, for defensive purposes, a large gauntlet of buff on the left arm, which covered it above the elbow. Its use, undoubtedly, was similar to that of the cloak or the shield, but we find very little reference to it in the works of the masters.

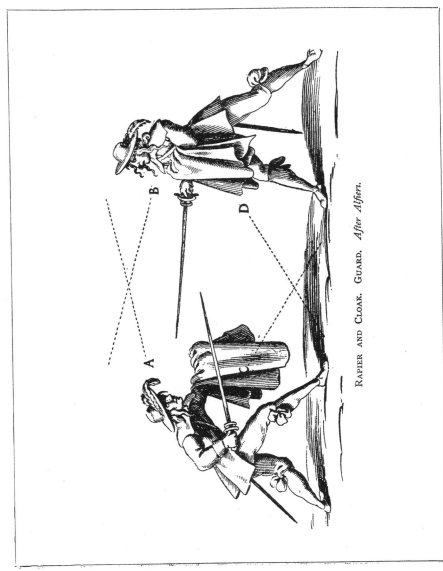

PLATE 30.

RAPIER AND CLOAK. GUARD. *After Alfieri.*

PLATE 31.

PARRY OF TIERCE AND RIPOSTE AT THROAT. *After Alfieri.*

Line A denotes a "riverso" at the head, B a thrust at the body, and C a "mandritto" at the leg.

PLATE 32.

THROWING THE CLOAK.   *After Alfieri.*

Line A denotes a "mandritto" at the head, and B a "riverso" at the arm.

CHAPTER VI.

DAGGER AND CLOAK.

THE Dagger used by Marozzo was the "Pugnale Bolognese," a large double-edged weapon, sufficiently heavy for cutting as well as thrusting.

He is most impressive on one very important point, namely, that as the dagger is a very short weapon, so it is an extremely dangerous one, and requires most careful watching, and that therefore the eyes must never be taken off the dagger-hand of the enemy. The cloak is worn and manipulated in much the same manner as when it accompanies the sword (Plate 33). Feints may be made with the dagger in order to gain openings, and, similarly, openings may be shown with the cloak for the purpose of drawing an attack, the parry and riposte having been already determined on. The following movements of dagger and cloak are extracts from Marozzo's work.

1. Hold your dagger in quarte (*coda lunga e stretta*), with the right foot leading, and keep your cloak rather low, in order to draw a mandritto at the head, or a high thrust; and

as the enemy does this, oppose the folds of your cloak to his dagger, pass forward the left foot, and give him a quarte thrust (*punta riverso*) in his right side.

Recover by passing the left foot back, and take the same guard as before.

2. Make a great oblique pass with your left foot outside his right, envelop his dagger-arm with your cloak, and deliver a thrust or a riverso at his neck.

Recover, passing back three or four paces, and take the same guard.

3. Lower your cloak and give an opening above, and as he attacks give a mandritto at his hand on the pass.

Recover, passing back the right foot.

4. Stand on guard in tierce, with the left foot advanced. Show an opening at your left side by carrying your cloak a little over towards your right, and when he attacks, force his dagger well over to your left, pass forward your right foot, and give either point or a riverso at his face.

Recover, retiring three or four paces.

PLATE 33.

DAGGER AND CLOAK. GUARD. *After Marozzo.*

CHAPTER VII.

THE CASE OF RAPIERS.

THIS consisted of an exact pair of swords, one for each hand, and they were kept together in one and the same scabbard; they were somewhat similar to those used in buckler-play. The study of this method of fence is recommended by Marozzo, Di Grassi, and others, for the reason that it is difficult, and is, moreover, very little understood, and might therefore be exceedingly useful in a serious fight in the lists.

According to Marozzo, the combatants engaged with the most advanced sword held in quarte, and the other in tierce (Plate 34); but Di Grassi advises a somewhat different attitude, the rear-ward sword being held in a sort of prime, while the other was kept low, with the hand a little in advance of the side (Plate 35). The position of Marozzo is perhaps the most preferable. Di Grassi lays much stress on "finding" and dominating with the advanced sword one or other of the enemy's weapons. The advanced sword was generally used for defence, and sometimes for feinting, while the real attack was made on the pass with the other sword.

The term "within" signifies the part in the middle, that is to say, between the two swords.

THE PARRIES.

The parries were practically the same as our modern ones, the main difference being in the names they were known by. In describing the play, therefore, I shall employ for the most part the names as at present understood. We have, then, sixte or tierce, and octave or seconde (the ancients used the true and false edge indiscriminately), to protect the outside; and quarte, septime, and, if need be, the primes to cover the inside.

The lessons of Marozzo for the Case of Rapiers are as follow :—

1. On guard. Left foot advanced. *Right sword* in tierce. *Left sword* in quarte.

M.	P.
Show an opening above *left sword*, and with *right sword* cut false edge under his left arm.	
	Parry seconde with *left sword*, and return point at his face with *right sword*.
Parry sixte with *left sword*, pass and point at his body with *right sword*.	

Recover by passing backwards, holding both your swords extended towards the enemy with their points crossing, and resume your guard.

PLATE 34.

"CASE OF RAPIERS." GUARD. *After Marozzo.*

PLATE 35.

"Case of Rapiers." Guard. *After Di Grassi.*

2. On guard as before.

M.	P.
Show an opening at left leg.	Cut a mandritto at the left thigh with the *right sword*.
Parry octave (or seconde) with *left sword*, and riposte, either mandritto at left cheek, "coup de Jarnac," or a point with *right sword*.	

N.B.—If P. cuts a riverso at the thigh, it must be parried with septime. Seconde is the best parry for the "coup de Jarnac."

3. To draw a riverso.　On guard as before.

M.	P.
Advance right foot.	Cut riverso (cut 4) at his right thigh with *right sword*.
Parry low prime with *left sword*, and with *right sword* give a riverso at his right cheek.	
Recover as before.	

4. On guard as before.

M.	P.
With *left sword* feint a thrust within, pass right foot, and give "Jarnac" with *right sword*.	
Recover as before.	Parry seconde with *left sword*.

5. On guard as before.

M.   P.

With *left sword* give riverso within at his left arm, pass right foot, and give with *right sword* either point at side or mandritto at leg.

Recover as before.

6. On guard as before.

M.   P.

Turn *left sword* to tierce and engage his left sword with it on the outside, feint with it a thrust over the sword at his head, pass and give a mandritto at his thigh with *right sword*.

Recover as before.   Parry seconde with *left sword.*

7. On guard as before.

M.   P.

Feint false edge at advanced hand with *left sword*, pass and give riverso at thigh with *right sword*.

                               Parry septime with *left sword*, and riposte riverso at right cheek with *right sword.*

Parry quarte with *left sword*, and give mandritto at left cheek with *right sword*.   Parry sixte with *left sword.*

Recover as before.

PLATE 36.

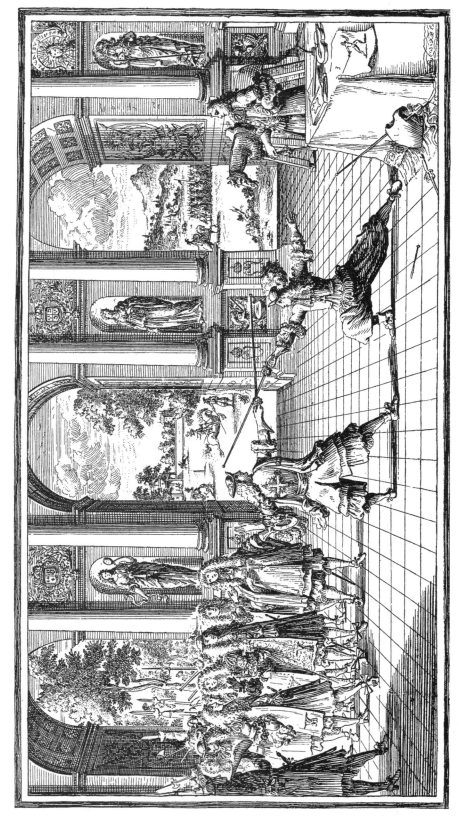

A "SALLE D'ARMES" IN THE SEVENTEENTH CENTURY. *After Philibert de la Touche, 1670.*

CHAPTER VIII.

THE TRANSITION PERIOD.

URING the first half of the seventeenth century the dagger, by degrees, became unfashionable as an article of costume, and in Western Europe, certainly, the rapier also underwent a change—it was sensibly curtailed in the matter of its length. Although the short sword (*épée courte*) was not generally adopted until about the year 1660, during the reign of Louis XIV., this revolution in the form of the weapon necessitated the invention, on the part of the French masters, of a new school of fence to suit the new arm. Of all the works on seventeenth-century fencing, that of Wernesson de Liancour, published in 1686, is the most typical. The fundamental rules of his art were very similar to our own modern ones, although something of the old rapier-play was retained, especially the recourse to the left hand for defence; while the swords were, many of them, so long and out of balance, that the masters actually taught their pupils to relieve the sword hand occasionally by taking hold

of the forte of the blade with the left, and thus manipu-
lating the weapon with both hands. (Plate 37.)

The Guard was something like that of the present day,
but the weight of the body was thrown entirely on the left
leg, with the right leg almost straight, the idea being to keep
as much out of reach as possible, while the left arm was
raised, as is ours; but it was much more curved, and the
hand was held near the face, and so directed towards the
front as to be in readiness for parrying if required. (Plate 38.)

The Parries were but four in number—quarte and tierce
for the high lines, with septime and seconde (under other
names) for the low ones. The counterparries had not yet
been invented.

The Attacks were also of a very simple kind, and consisted
of disengaging, beating on the blade, and such compound
attacks as " one, two," " over and under," and " under and
over."

The Lunge, in the early stages of small sword fencing,
possessed the defect of throwing the body very much forward,
in the hope of gaining a little more reach; and this was
exaggerated to such a degree as to cause the left foot to roll
over completely, the sole of the foot losing its contact with
the ground (Plate 42.)

The Pass in the seventeenth century was of two kinds.
The ordinary pass, which was effected by stepping forward
with the rearward foot and bringing it a full pace in front
of the other, was used for the purpose of approaching the
enemy, in order to seize either his person or his sword, or
occasionally to make a thrust. (Plate 40.) The other, which
we must term the *full pass*, was effected by stepping forward
so far with the rearward foot as to bring it, when the movement

PLATE 37.

HOLDING THE SWORD WITH BOTH HANDS. *After De Liancour.*

PLATE 38.

THE GUARD. *After De Liancour.*

was completed, into the position of a kind of lunge. It was extremely dangerous, and by the end of the century it had disappeared from the French School altogether. (Plate 41.)

The passes were met by certain counter-movements of the feet, consisting of a similar pass to the front or a pass to the rear, known as *counterpasses*, or a species of pass to one side, known as the *demivolte* and the *volte*. These latter were sometimes employed against a true lunge, but in that case it was usual to " oppose " the left hand to the enemy's blade during the execution of the movement.

The Demivolte was effected by straightening the legs and passing the left foot a quarter of a circle backwards towards the right, and turning on the toes of the right foot, by which means the trunk was carried out of the line, the head was turned towards the enemy, and the sword arm was straightened so as to receive him on the point. (Plate 42.)

The Volte was a more complete turn of the body, and was effected like the demivolte ; but the left foot described very nearly a half-circle, so that the back was half turned to the enemy, and the trunk was removed so entirely off the line that the opposition of the left hand was unnecessary. (Plate 41.)

SEIZURE OF BOTH SWORD AND PERSON.

Before we leave De Liancour we must note his curious advice on the method of treatment for one who rushes in with the intention of stabbing. As he encloses make a complete volte with the left foot, which will leave your right foot in front of you, and immediately pass back your right foot, placing it in rear of both his feet ; and during the

execution of this you exchange your sword into your left
hand, holding it by the middle of the blade, and presenting
the point at his throat; at the same time pass your right
hand across his body, and seize the shell of his sword.
(Plate 43.)

PLATE 39.

The Lunge. *After De la Touche.*

PLATE 40.

PASS AND VOLTE. *After De Liancour.*

PLATE 41.

THE FULL PASS.   *After De Liancour.*

PLATE 42.

LUNGE AND DEMIVOLTE. *After De Liancour.*

PLATE 43.

SEIZURE OF BOTH SWORD AND PERSON. *After De Liancour.*

CHAPTER IX.

THE EIGHTEENTH CENTURY.

E now approach the third period of our art; in which we find the walking sword, still the constant companion of the gentleman, gradually improving both in form and in lightness, until it reached its perfection about the middle of the eighteenth century, while the method of using it developed correspondingly. To form a correct idea of the style of this period, we may refer at once to the famous oblong folio brought out in 1763 by the first of the Angelos, though it is true that all the actual material found in that work occurs in others slightly earlier, and notably in the interesting "Nouveau Traité" of Girard, which appeared in 1737.

Under these masters we renew the acquaintance of the prime parry, in the form in which it is still sometimes used. We are introduced to a "feather parade" of "quarte over the arm" with the hand in supination, similar to our "sixte." We recognise the ancient parries for the low lines under the names of "seconde" and "half-circle" (the modern "septime"), and the parry of "quinte," which we now call "octave";

while movements practically the same as our counter-parries had been introduced under the name of " parades with a counter-disengage." In fact the fundamental principles of the art have, since the time of Angelo, scarcely been altered at all, while the academic gracefulness displayed in this and in many other contemporary works has certainly, at least, not been surpassed by modern swordsmen.

The movements of the eighteenth century most interesting from a dramatic point of view are the " salute " and the various methods of seizing the sword, given by Angelo, together with one or two of a more rough-and-ready description recommended by a German author named Weischner; and in giving the necessary explanations we cannot do better than use the words of the famous master himself:—

" THE SALUTE IN FENCING, GENERALLY MADE USE OF IN ALL ACADEMIES AMONG GENTLEMEN BEFORE THEY ASSAULT OR FENCE LOOSE.

" The salute in fencing is a civility due to the spectators, and reciprocally to the persons who are to fence. It is customary to begin with it before they engage. A genteel deportment and a graceful air are absolutely necessary to execute this.

" FIRST POSITION OF THE SALUTE.

" You must stand on your guard in tierce, and, engaging the feeble of your adversary's sword, make three beats of the foot, called attacks, two of which are made with the heel, and the third with the whole flat of the foot.

" Carry your left hand gracefully to your hat without stirring the head, which is to face the adversary ; and the hat being off, you must observe the following rules. (Plate 44.)

" SECOND POSITION OF THE SALUTE.

" You must pass your right foot behind the left at about a foot distance ; keep the knees strait, the body strait, and the head very erect ; at the same time stretch out your right arm and turn your wrist in carte, raising it to the height of your head, as much to the right as possible, holding the point a little low. When you pass the right foot behind the left you must drop and stretch your left arm, holding your hat with the hollow upwards, about two feet from your thigh. (Plate 45.)

" THIRD POSITION OF THE SALUTE.

" When you have saluted to the right, observe well that the wrist be carried to the left, bending the elbow, and keeping the point of your sword in line to the adversary's right shoulder. All the other parts of the body should be in the same position as before mentioned. (Plate 46.)

" FOURTH POSITION OF THE SALUTE.

" When the salute is made to the left, the wrist must be gracefully turned in tierce, holding the arm and the point of the sword in a line with the adversary, and at the same time come to your guard, by carrying the left leg about two feet distance from the right ; and bending the left arm, put on the hat in an easy and genteel manner, and place the hand in the position of guard. (Plate 47.)

" Fifth Position of the Salute.

" Being thus engaged in the position of your tierce guard, you must repeat the three attacks, or beats of the foot, and straitening your knees, pass your left foot forward, point outward, the heel about two inches distant from the point of the right foot, and, straitening both arms, turn both hands in carte, the left arm about two feet from the left thigh, the right arm in a line with the right eye, and the point of your sword in a line to your adversary. (Plate 48.)

" *Note.*—These last motions are to salute the adversary.

" After this last attitude you must come to your guard again, in what position of the wrist you please, either to attack or receive the adversary.

" If you should find yourself too near your adversary, after having made your pass forward with your left foot, you should immediately carry your left foot back, and come to your guard, to shun an expected surprise."

THE DISARMS BY SEIZING THE SWORD.

" Of a Disarm after having Parried the Carte Thrust.

" If the adversary is irregular and careless when he thrusts a carte, you should parry him with the carte parade, by a dry, smart beat with your forte, seize the shell of his sword with your left hand, bring up your left leg to the right, and with the forte of your sword bear strong on his blade, which will oblige him to open his fingers, and drawing in your arm, still holding his sword fast, you will become master thereof. (Plate 49.) The disarm being made, carry your left foot two feet back with a straight knee, and present the two points at him. (Plate 50.)

THE SALUTE: FIRST POSITION.   *After Angelo.*

PLATE 45.

THE SALUTE: SECOND POSITION. *After Angelo.*

PLATE 46.

THE SALUTE: THIRD POSITION.   *After Angelo.*

PLATE 47.

THE SALUTE: FOURTH POSITION. *After Angelo.*

PLATE 48.

THE SALUTE: FIFTH POSITION.   *After Angelo.*

PLATE 49.

83

A DISARM AFTER HAVING PARRIED QUARTE: FIRST POSITION. *After Angelo.*

PLATE 50.

A Disarm after having parried Quarte : Second Position. *After Angelo.*

" Of the Disarm on the Thrust in Tierce, or Carte
over the Arm.

" If the adversary makes a thrust in tierce, or carte over
the arm, and abandons his body in a careless manner, you
must parry him by a dry, smart beat with the edge of your
forte, traversing the line of the blade, and force or bear his
wrist upwards, at the same time passing the left foot about
a foot before the right ; still holding fast his sword, you
should throw his arm outward to the right, and carry your left
foot forward about two feet (Plate 51) ; bending your right
knee, and straightening the left, present the point of your
sword to his face. (Plate 52.)

" Of the Disarm on the Carte, or Seconde Thrust, after
having Parried with the Prime Parade.

" If you are engaged in tierce, make an attack of the foot,
and force the enemy's blade on the outside to excite him to
thrust ; and at the time that he thrusts either carte or seconde,
parry quickly with the prime, and advance about half a foot, and
with swiftness pass your left arm over the forte of his blade ;
by this means, by drawing in your body and left arm, he will
be forced to quit his sword (Plate 53) ; as soon as the disarm
is made, present your point, and pass swiftly back, with your
right foot distant from the left as you will see in Plate 54.

" Of the Disarm after the Parade on the Outside of
the Sword.

" If you are engaged on the outside, either in tierce or
carte over the arm, you must make an appel of the foot, and
force or bear a little on his blade to excite him to thrust a
carte within the sword.

" At the time he disengages and thrusts out, you must

counter-disengage and parry, forcing his blade upwards with
the forte of yours; you are to pass your left foot before the
right about the distance of a foot, and with liveliness and
resolution with your left hand seize the shell of his sword;
and as in defending himself he might bring up his left leg and
throw himself forward on the blade, to hinder his seizing it
you should instantly throw your right shoulder and arm back
and carry your right foot behind the left about a foot, and turning the point of your left foot facing his knee, and passing your
sword behind your back, leaving your wrist against your loins,
present the point of your sword to his belly." (Plate 55.)

The German, Weischner, whose work appeared in 1765,
gives us two curious methods of overpowering an enemy. In
the first (Plate 56) the assailant has attempted a thrust in
seconde on the pass, the defender has avoided this by a
counter-pass, opposing his sword to that of the enemy in so
doing, and on the completion of this counter-pass he has forced
him forward by pressing the forte of his sword on the back
part of his neck, at the same time seizing his right leg, and
so throwing him to the ground.

The second seizure of Weischner (Plate 57) was effected
when the enemy had attempted to deliver a thrust in
tierce over the arm on the pass. The defender has here
parried tierce, has made a counter-pass with his left foot, at
the same time bearing down the sword of the assailant; he
has then, by bringing up his right foot, placed himself behind
him, and has passed his left arm across his breast, by means
of which he is depicted in the act of throwing him backward.

Such are the leading features of the Fence of the eighteenth
century, the end of which period brings us face to face with
the art as it is practised at the present time.

A Disarm after having parried Tierce: First Position. *After Angelo.*

PLATE 52.

PLATE 53.

A Disarm after having parried Prime: First Position. *After Angelo.*

PLATE 54.

A Disarm after having parried Prime: Second Position. *After Angelo.*

A Disarm after the Parry on the Outside of the Sword. *After Angelo.*

PLATE 56.

Seizure and Forward Throw. *After Weischner.*

PLATE 57.

Seizure and Backward Throw. *After Weischner.*

A CATALOG OF SELECTED

DOVER BOOKS

IN ALL FIELDS OF INTEREST

A CATALOG OF SELECTED DOVER
BOOKS IN ALL FIELDS OF INTEREST

CONCERNING THE SPIRITUAL IN ART, Wassily Kandinsky. Pioneering work by father of abstract art. Thoughts on color theory, nature of art. Analysis of earlier masters. 12 illustrations. 80pp. of text. 5⅜ x 8½.   23411-8

ANIMALS: 1,419 Copyright-Free Illustrations of Mammals, Birds, Fish, Insects, etc., Jim Harter (ed.). Clear wood engravings present, in extremely lifelike poses, over 1,000 species of animals. One of the most extensive pictorial sourcebooks of its kind. Captions. Index. 284pp. 9 x 12.   23766-4

CELTIC ART: The Methods of Construction, George Bain. Simple geometric techniques for making Celtic interlacements, spirals, Kells-type initials, animals, humans, etc. Over 500 illustrations. 160pp. 9 x 12. (Available in U.S. only.)   22923-8

AN ATLAS OF ANATOMY FOR ARTISTS, Fritz Schider. Most thorough reference work on art anatomy in the world. Hundreds of illustrations, including selections from works by Vesalius, Leonardo, Goya, Ingres, Michelangelo, others. 593 illustrations. 192pp. 7⅛ x 10¼.   20241-0

CELTIC HAND STROKE-BY-STROKE (Irish Half-Uncial from "The Book of Kells"): An Arthur Baker Calligraphy Manual, Arthur Baker. Complete guide to creating each letter of the alphabet in distinctive Celtic manner. Covers hand position, strokes, pens, inks, paper, more. Illustrated. 48pp. 8¼ x 11.   24336-2

EASY ORIGAMI, John Montroll. Charming collection of 32 projects (hat, cup, pelican, piano, swan, many more) specially designed for the novice origami hobbyist. Clearly illustrated easy-to-follow instructions insure that even beginning papercrafters will achieve successful results. 48pp. 8¼ x 11.   27298-2

THE COMPLETE BOOK OF BIRDHOUSE CONSTRUCTION FOR WOODWORKERS, Scott D. Campbell. Detailed instructions, illustrations, tables. Also data on bird habitat and instinct patterns. Bibliography. 3 tables. 63 illustrations in 15 figures. 48pp. 5¼ x 8½.   24407-5

BLOOMINGDALE'S ILLUSTRATED 1886 CATALOG: Fashions, Dry Goods and Housewares, Bloomingdale Brothers. Famed merchants' extremely rare catalog depicting about 1,700 products: clothing, housewares, firearms, dry goods, jewelry, more. Invaluable for dating, identifying vintage items. Also, copyright-free graphics for artists, designers. Co-published with Henry Ford Museum & Greenfield Village. 160pp. 8¼ x 11.   25780-0

HISTORIC COSTUME IN PICTURES, Braun & Schneider. Over 1,450 costumed figures in clearly detailed engravings–from dawn of civilization to end of 19th century. Captions. Many folk costumes. 256pp. 8⅜ x 11¾.   23150-X

THE STORY OF THE TITANIC AS TOLD BY ITS SURVIVORS, Jack Winocour (ed.). What it was really like. Panic, despair, shocking inefficiency, and a little heroism. More thrilling than any fictional account. 26 illustrations. 320pp. 5⅜ x 8½. 20610-6

FAIRY AND FOLK TALES OF THE IRISH PEASANTRY, William Butler Yeats (ed.). Treasury of 64 tales from the twilight world of Celtic myth and legend: "The Soul Cages," "The Kildare Pooka," "King O'Toole and his Goose," many more. Introduction and Notes by W. B. Yeats. 352pp. 5⅜ x 8½. 26941-8

BUDDHIST MAHAYANA TEXTS, E. B. Cowell and others (eds.). Superb, accurate translations of basic documents in Mahayana Buddhism, highly important in history of religions. The Buddha-karita of Asvaghosha, Larger Sukhavativyuha, more. 448pp. 5⅜ x 8½. 25552-2

ONE TWO THREE . . . INFINITY: Facts and Speculations of Science, George Gamow. Great physicist's fascinating, readable overview of contemporary science: number theory, relativity, fourth dimension, entropy, genes, atomic structure, much more. 128 illustrations. Index. 352pp. 5⅜ x 8½. 25664-2

EXPERIMENTATION AND MEASUREMENT, W. J. Youden. Introductory manual explains laws of measurement in simple terms and offers tips for achieving accuracy and minimizing errors. Mathematics of measurement, use of instruments, experimenting with machines. 1994 edition. Foreword. Preface. Introduction. Epilogue. Selected Readings. Glossary. Index. Tables and figures. 128pp. 5⅜ x 8½. 40451-X

DALÍ ON MODERN ART: The Cuckolds of Antiquated Modern Art, Salvador Dalí. Influential painter skewers modern art and its practitioners. Outrageous evaluations of Picasso, Cézanne, Turner, more. 15 renderings of paintings discussed. 44 calligraphic decorations by Dalí. 96pp. 5⅜ x 8½. (Available in U.S. only.) 29220-7

ANTIQUE PLAYING CARDS: A Pictorial History, Henry René D'Allemagne. Over 900 elaborate, decorative images from rare playing cards (14th–20th centuries): Bacchus, death, dancing dogs, hunting scenes, royal coats of arms, players cheating, much more. 96pp. 9¼ x 12¼. 29265-7

MAKING FURNITURE MASTERPIECES: 30 Projects with Measured Drawings, Franklin H. Gottshall. Step-by-step instructions, illustrations for constructing handsome, useful pieces, among them a Sheraton desk, Chippendale chair, Spanish desk, Queen Anne table and a William and Mary dressing mirror. 224pp. 8⅛ x 11¼. 29338-6

THE FOSSIL BOOK: A Record of Prehistoric Life, Patricia V. Rich et al. Profusely illustrated definitive guide covers everything from single-celled organisms and dinosaurs to birds and mammals and the interplay between climate and man. Over 1,500 illustrations. 760pp. 7½ x 10⅛. 29371-8

Paperbound unless otherwise indicated. Available at your book dealer, online at **www.doverpublications.com**, or by writing to Dept. GI, Dover Publications, Inc., 31 East 2nd Street, Mineola, NY 11501. For current price information or for free catalogues (please indicate field of interest), write to Dover Publications or log on to **www.doverpublications.com** and see every Dover book in print. Dover publishes more than 500 books each year on science, elementary and advanced mathematics, biology, music, art, literary history, social sciences, and other areas.